Contents

Some words are shown in bold, **like this**. You can find out what they mean by looking in the Glossary.

Nature's shapes

Flowers and plants grow into all sorts of shapes.

They can be smooth or spiked, bent or straight.

They may have a **circle** or **triangle** shape.

These natural shapes can be found all around us.

Can you see any star, circle or triangle shapes in the picture?

2-D four-sided shapes

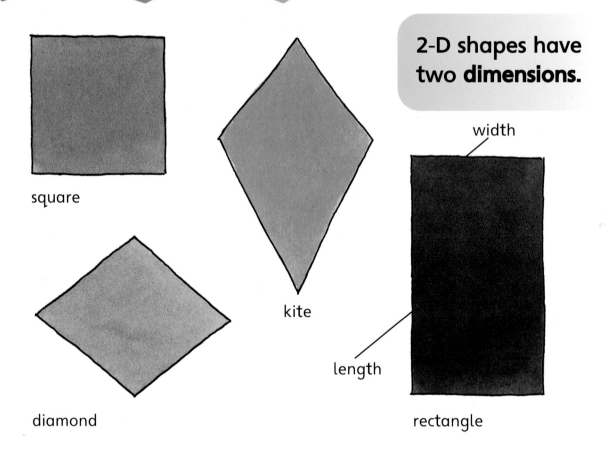

2-D shapes have two **dimensions.**

square

kite

width

length

diamond

rectangle

2-D shapes are flat. They have length and width, but no thickness. The 2-D shapes you can see here have four sides. Their special names are **square**, **rectangle**, **diamond** and **kite**.

6

A square has four equal sides.

You can find four-sided shapes everywhere. They are very common.

Look at the picture of different four-sided shapes. Some of them have special names. How many can you name?

2-D three-sided shapes

Some **2-D** shapes have three sides. They are called
triangles. Although they may look different,
every triangle has three straight sides. There is an
angle at each of the pointed corners.

You can find triangles in all sorts of places. Sometimes things are nearly triangles but not quite. They might have rounded corners or a **curved** side.

Look at this picture. Can you find some shapes that are nearly triangles?

Curved 2-D shapes

Shapes can have **curves**. They can also have curves and straight lines. Some curved shapes have special names such as **circle**, **semicircle**, **oval** and **heart**.

10

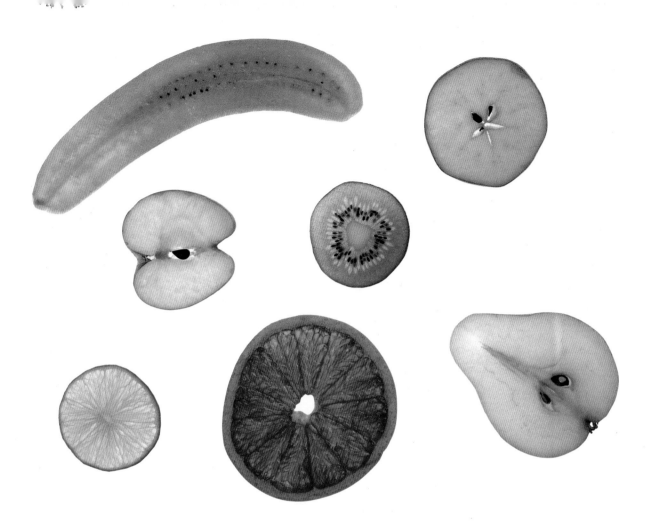

We see examples of shapes with curved sides all around us. Some curved shapes can also have points or corners.

Look at the pictures. Which fruit do you think each slice comes from?

Many-sided shapes

Any shape with straight sides is a **polygon**. Some polygons have special names such as **triangle, square, rectangle, pentagon** or **hexagon**. Even if the sides point inwards, they are still polygons.

12

We can see different kinds of polygons everywhere.
Some have three sides, some four, some five
(pentagons), some six (hexagons), and so on.

Look at the picture. Can you find four special
polygons you can name?

3-D shapes

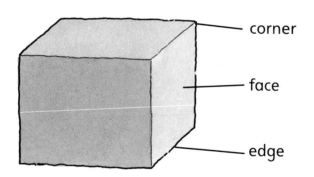

corner

face

edge

3-D shapes have three **dimensions**. They have length, width and thickness or height.

3-D shapes have thickness. They have length, width and height. In the picture, most of the faces on the 3-D shapes are **rectangles** or **squares**.

14

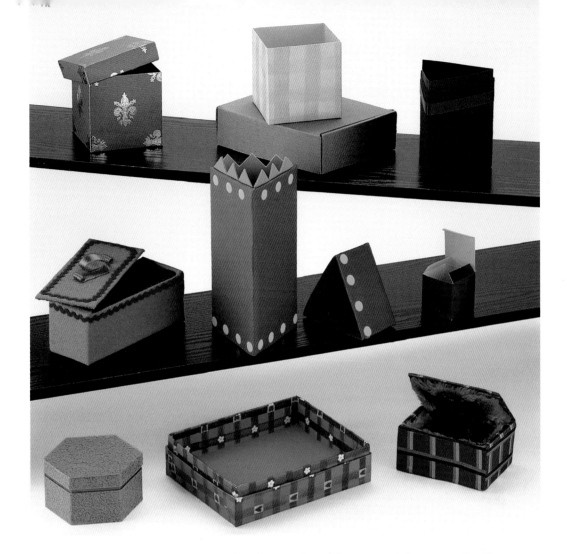

3-D shapes can be solid or **hollow**. These 3-D shapes all have some faces which are rectangles or squares.

Look at the ends of these shapes. Can you name which **polygon** shape they are?

Curved 3-D shapes

cylinders

cones

spheres

Some **3-D** shapes have **curved** faces. Perfectly round shapes, like balls, are **spheres**. Shapes like tubes, with **circles** at each end, are **cylinders**. **Cones** have a circle at one end and a point at the other.

3-D shapes with curves may be **hollow** or **solid**.
Some have flat faces as well as curved faces.
Because the shapes have curves, they will roll.

Which curved shape will roll the best?

17

3-D triangles

pyramids with **square, triangle** or **hexagon bases.**

Some **3-D** shapes have **triangle** faces. Shapes with a **polygon** end or base, and with triangle faces going to a point, are called **pyramids**.

18

Look carefully and you will find shapes which have triangle faces. Sometimes every face is a triangle, but not always.

Look at the picture. How many pyramids can you see?

Shape bits

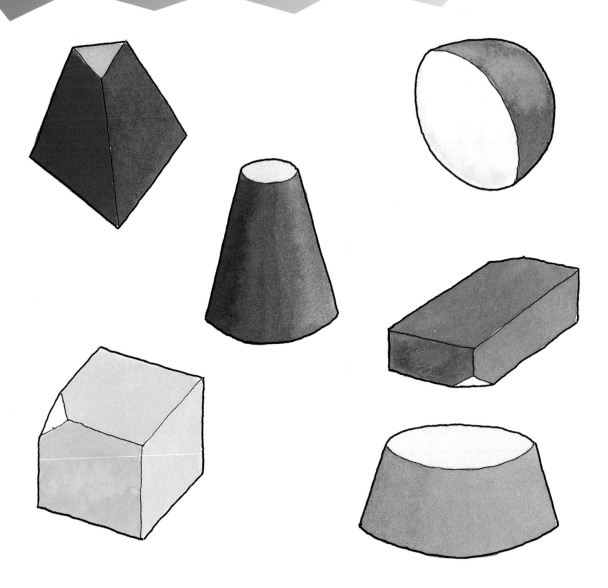

Sometimes part of a shape may be missing.

It may be half of the shape or just a corner.

Bits are cut from shapes for all sorts of reasons.

Look at the shapes made when bits are cut off these cheeses. Do the new shapes look like the whole cheeses they were cut from?

New shapes

Two or more shapes can be fitted together to make a new shape. The picture shows how this can be done.

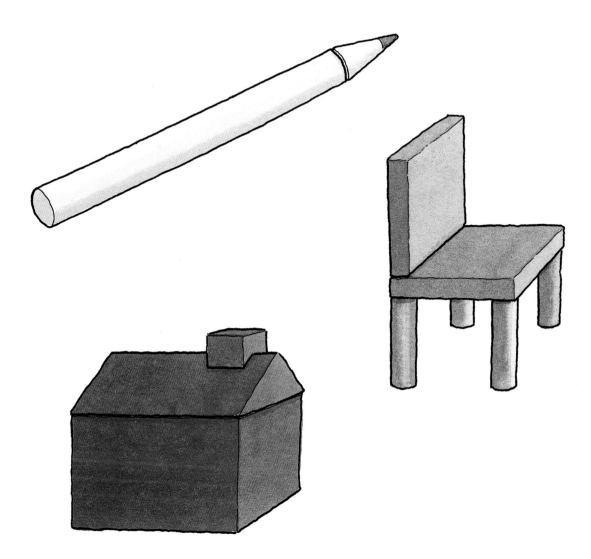

Everyday shapes are often two or more other shapes put together.

Look at the picture. What shapes are these things made from?

Fitting shapes together

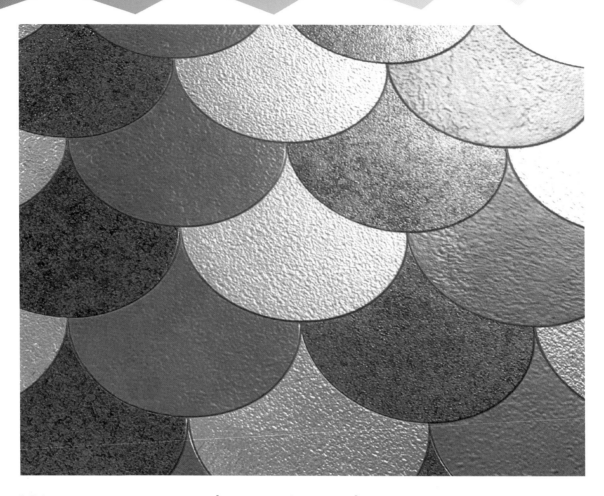

We can arrange shapes to make a pattern. If the pattern has no gaps or holes, we say the shapes **tessellate**. Tessellating is putting shapes together without leaving gaps.

We can tessellate with **3-D** shapes. When shapes are put together as close as possible, they take up the least space.

These things have been neatly stacked. Which shapes do you think tessellate?

Same shape

When a shape is **rotated**, or flipped over, it may look different. Its position changes but nothing else. It is still the same shape. There are matching pairs of shapes in the picture.

We often need to find matching shapes. Spotting shapes that have been turned around is not always very easy.

Can you find where each jigsaw piece will fit?

Symmetry

When some shapes are folded in half, the two
halves match. When this happens, the shape
is **symmetrical**.

Reflections in a flat mirror make an exact copy. The object and its reflection make a symmetrical pattern.

Take a simple object and hold it close to a mirror. Can you see the symmetrical pattern it makes?

Glossary

angle the corner of a polygon

circle perfectly round 2-D shape

cone 3-D shape with a circle at one end and a point at the other

curved lines which are not straight

cylinder 3-D shape like a tube with circle ends

diamond 4-sided shape. Its sides are the same length.

dimension the length, width and height of a shape are its dimensions. See also 2-D and 3-D.

heart shape like a heart

hexagon 2-D shape which has 6 straight sides

hollow empty or having nothing inside

kite 2-D shape with 4 sides. Looks like a kite.

oval a round 2-D shape which is longer than it is wide

pentagon 2-D shape which has 5 straight sides

polygon any 2-D shape which has straight sides

pyramid 3-D shape with triangle sides and a polygon base. The sides come to a point.

rectangle 2-D 4-sided shape. Its opposite sides are the same length and its 4 angles are the same size.

reflection the picture you see in a mirror

rotate to turn a shape round

semicircle half of a circle

solid 3-D shape

sphere a perfectly round shape, like a ball

square 4-sided shape. Its sides are the same length and it has 4 right angles.

symmetrical a balanced shape or picture. One half will fold exactly over the other half.

tessellate fit shapes together without leaving any gaps

3-D shape any shape with 3 dimensions: length, width and thickness or height

triangle 2-D shape which has 3 sides

2-D shape any shape with only 2 dimensions: length and width. It does not have thickness.

31

Answers

Index